The Caspall Family of Kent England

by Lorine McGinnis Schulze

ISBN: 978-1-987938-15-9
Copyright 2017
All rights reserved
Publisher Olive Tree Genealogy

Over the last 40 plus years I have researched and gathered a great deal of information and uncovered many documents for my mother's ancestors in England. Pondering how best to preserve my research and share the stories of these maternal ancestors, I decided to compile books on each family surname.

Because the books were written for family, I have not cited my sources nor have I written long chapters of anecdotal stories. Instead I opted to create a chronological timeline for each generation. Images for all baptismal, marriage, burial, land records and so on that were discovered for each ancestor are also included.

If siblings were found, family group sheets are included. If they were not found, only my direct ancestor is noted. At the end of the book you will find blank pages for your own notes.

Those who want to know my sources can contact me directly through my website Olive Tree Genealogy at www.OliveTreeGenealogy.com My email is found at the bottom of each page.

I hope that readers enjoy these books and the stories of the ancestors.

Lorine McGinnis Schulze

Table of Contents

Caspall Family

My Caspall family dates back to John Caspall born ca 1717 in Stonar Kent England. He and his wife Mary Prigg lived out their lives in Sandwich Kent which is only a few miles from Stonar.

The Caspall line daughtered out for me with the birth of Mary Ann Norman Caspall in 1870 in Ramsgate, Kent. Mary Ann Norman was my great-grandmother and she married Charles Fuller.

Most of my Caspall ancestors were shipwrights and fishermen who plied their trade up and down the east coast of England.

John Caspall 1717-1744

The first record found for John is his marriage to Mary Prigg on 20 November 1737 in St. Clements, Sandwich Kent England.

John is recorded as being from Stonar, and may refer to Stonar Close just outside of Ramsgate. However there was also a Stonar Close on the outskirts of Sandwich. They married nine months after the birth of their first child, my 6th great-grandfather John.

John and Mary's second son William was baptised in 1740 at St. Clements and once again John and Mary were recorded as being from Stonar. He was also listed as living in Stonar at the baptism of his daughter Mary in 1744.

Two months after their daughter Mary was born, John Caspall was buried at St. Clements. His date of burial was 11 July 1744 and his cause of death from smallpox was recorded. It is unusual for a cause of death to be recorded so we might assume that smallpox was a terrifying and extremely contagious disease that could spread like wildfire through a village. On this same page in the church register it was noted that a "Wm. George, a stranger" had also died of smallpox a few days after John Caspall was buried. No doubt Mr. George carried the disease with him when he came to the village.

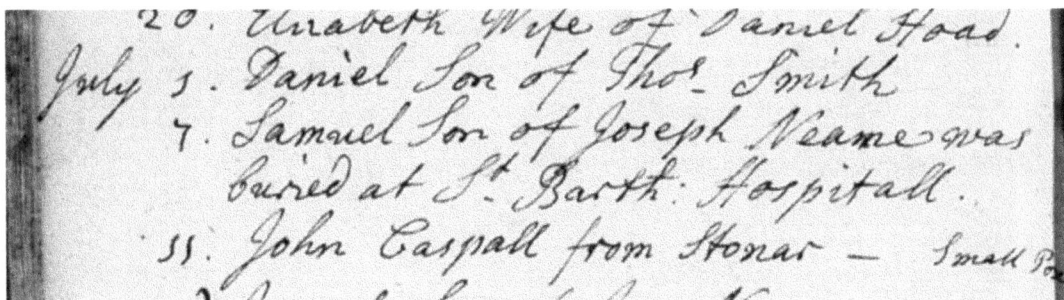

Mary (Prigg) Caspall was buried at St. Clements on 1 March 1746. She was noted as being a widow. Her children were left orphans – John age 9, William age 6 and little

Mary only 2 years old. It appears Mary may have had another son, also named William, who died 02 Oct 1746 and was buried in St. Clements. He is recorded only as "an infant". It is unlikey the term would be used for a 6 year old so this is most likely not the William born in 1740.

Family Group Sheet for John Caspall

Husband:		John Caspall
	b:	Bef. 1717 in Stonar, Kent England
	m:	20 Nov 1737 in Sandwich, St. Clements, Kent
	d:	11 Jul 1744 in Sandwich, St. Clements, Kent
	Father:	
	Mother:	
Wife:		Mary Prigg
	d:	01 Mar 1746 in Sandwich, St. Clements, Kent
	Father:	
	Mother:	
Children:		
1	Name:	John Caspall
M	b:	29 Jan 1737 in Sandwich, St. Clements, Kent
	m:	07 Nov 1757 in Kennington, Kent England
	d:	06 Sep 1801 in Sandwich, St. Clements, Kent
	Spouse:	Sarah Austin
2	Name:	William Caspall
M	b:	21 Sep 1740 in Sandwich, St. Clements, Kent
3	Name:	Mary Caspall
F	b:	13 May 1744 in Sandwich, St. Clements, Kent
4	Name:	William Caspall
M	b:	1746
	d:	02 Oct 1746 in Sandwich, St. Clements, Kent

John Caspall 1737-1801

John Caspall , my 6th great-grandfather, was born circa 1737. His banns of marriage to Sarah Austin took place in Kennington on 16 October 1757. At this time he was living in the parish of Lydd. They married in Kennington, which is only 20 miles from Lydd, on 7 November 1757. Less than one month later their son James, my 5th great-grandfather, was born.

It is likely that John was the child baptised in Sandwich, St Clement on 29 January 1737 to John and Mary (Prigg) Caspall. You will notice that in the church register the word "Sojourner" is written beside the baptism. That means either father, mother, or both parents were from a different parish.

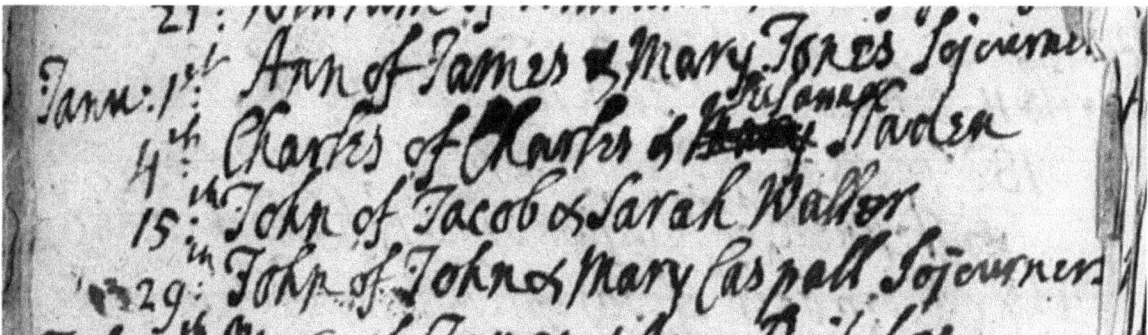

John's burial took place in Sandwich St. Clements on 06 Sep 1801. He is noted as a labourer, his age was given as 61 and a notation in the register reads "from St. Mary's"

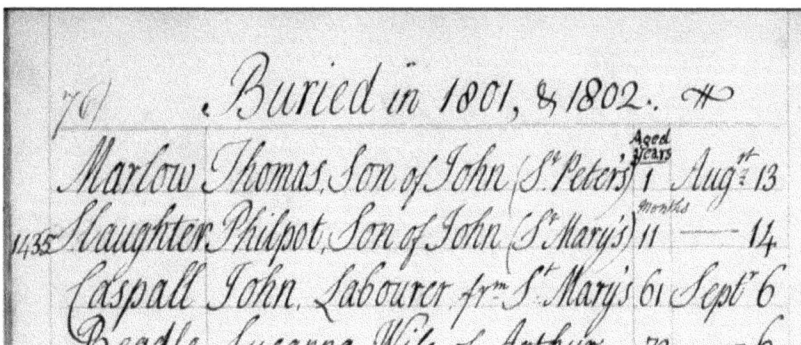

Family Group Sheet for John Caspall

Husband:		John Caspall
	b:	29 Jan 1737 in Sandwich, St. Clements, Kent
	m:	07 Nov 1757 in Kennington, Kent England
	d:	06 Sep 1801 in Sandwich, St. Clements, Kent
	Father:	John Caspall
	Mother:	Mary Prigg
Wife:		Sarah Austin
	Father:	
	Mother:	
Children:		
1	Name:	James Caspall
M	b:	11 Dec 1757 in Kennngton Kent England
	m:	01 Jan 1780 in Folkestone, Kent Eng
	d:	01 Jul 1812 in Dover, England
	Spouse:	Sarah Peerless
2	Name:	William Caspall
M	b:	29 Nov 1759 in Charlton, Kent, England

James Caspall 1757-1812

My 5th great-grandfather James Caspall was baptised December 11, 1757 in Kennington Kent England to John and Sarah Caspall. His parents had only been married one month when James was born.

On December 5, 1779 James married Sarah Peerlees in St Mary & St. Eanswith in Folkestone Kent. Folkestone is 16 miles from Kennington. They were both recorded as being from that Parish. Daniel Pearless [sic] was a witness but his relationship to Sarah is not known.

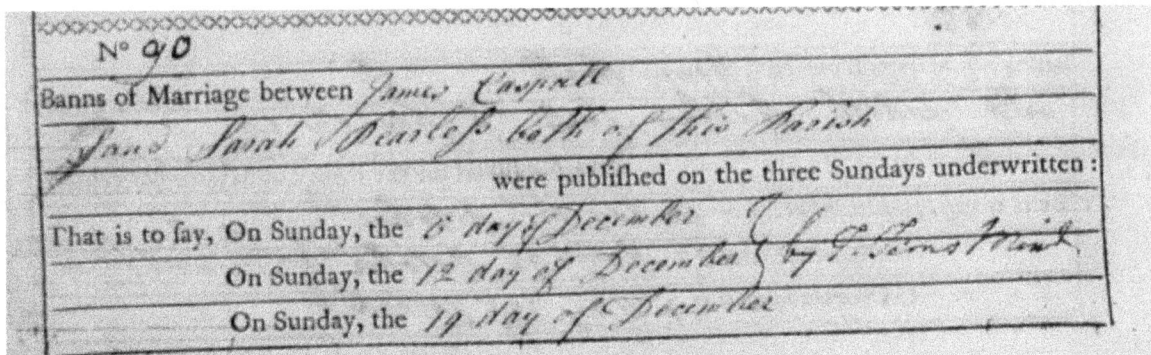
Figure 1: 1779 Banns of Marriage James Caspall to Sarah Peerless

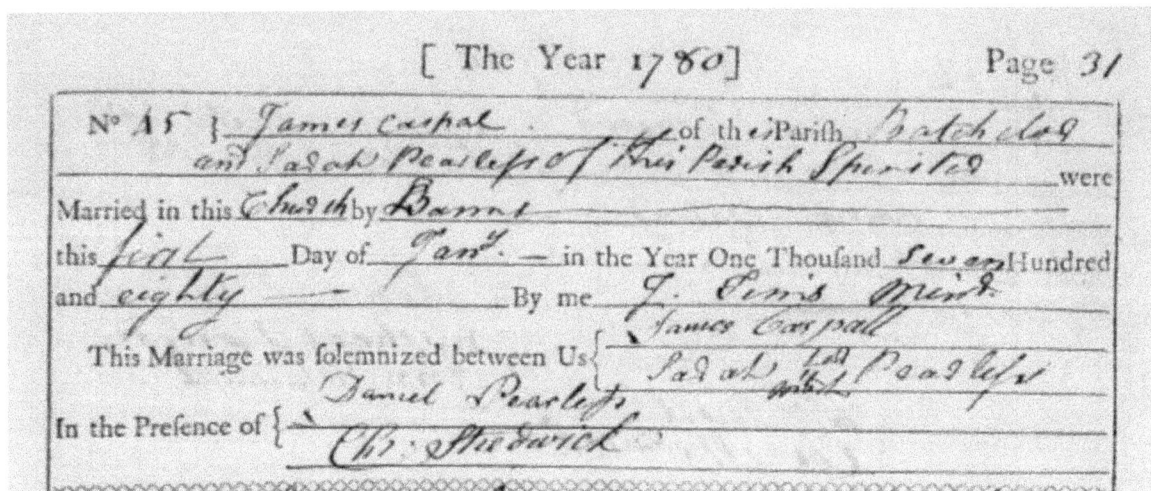
Figure 2: 1780 Marriage James Caspall to Sarah Peerlees

Church where John Caspall & Sarah Peerless married.
By Poliphilo - Own work, CC0,
https://commons.wikimedia.org/w/index.php?curid=46108257

Sarah Caspall's burial is found in St. Mary the Virgin Church Records in Dover Kent on April 13, 1834. She was 72 years old

Figure 3: Burial Sarah Caspall 1834

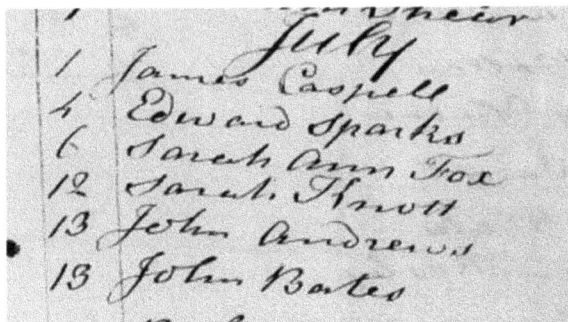

James Caspall was buried in the same church 22 years earlier, on 01 July 1812. No information is given in the burial record, not even his age.

Figure 4: 1812 Burial James Caspall in Dover

We believe that Sarah may be the Sarah Peerless born 6 February 1758 and baptised 19 February that year in Newington next Hythe, St Nicholas to parents Thomas and Mary Peerless. Proof is still being sought but I have tentatively linked her in this family group.

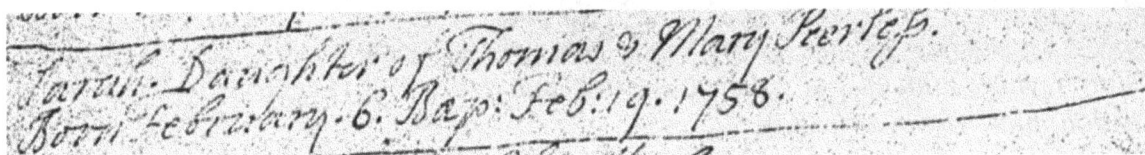

Family Group Sheet for James Caspall

Husband:		James Caspall
	b:	11 Dec 1757 in Kennngton Kent England
	m:	01 Jan 1780 in Folkestone, Kent Eng
	d:	01 Jul 1812 in Dover, England
	Father:	John Caspall
	Mother:	Sarah Austin
Wife:		Sarah Peerless
	b:	06 Feb 1758 in Newington next Hythe, St Nicholas, Kent
	d:	13 Apr 1834 in Dover, Kent
	Father:	Thomas Peerless
	Mother:	Mary Hutchford
Children:		
1	Name:	John Caspall
M	b:	02 Apr 1780 in Folkestone, Kent Eng
	m:	06 Jun 1805 in St. Laurence, Ramsgate, Kent Eng.
	d:	31 Oct 1852 in Ramsgate, Kent Eng
	Spouse:	Milly Elizabeth Hubbard
2	Name:	James Caspall
M	b:	10 Mar 1782 in Folkestone, Kent
	d:	22 Aug 1784 in Folkestone, Kent, Eng
3	Name:	Elizabeth Caspall
F	b:	21 Jan 1787 in Folkestone, Kent

John Caspall 1780-1852

John was baptised 2 April 1780 in Folkstone, Kent England. His parents were recorded in the church register of St Mary & Eanswith as James & Sarah Caspall

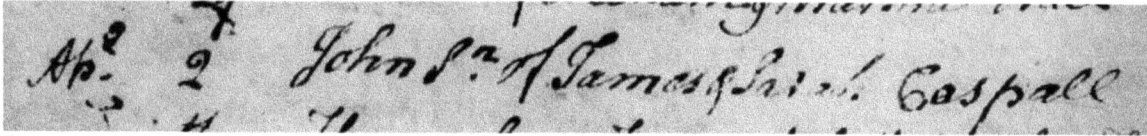

Figure 5: Baptism John Caspall 1780

On 6 June 1805 John married Milly Elizabeth Hubbard in St. Laurence of Thanet. Witnesses at marriage of John and Milley Elizabeth, both of St. Lawrence, were James Goss and Margaret Hubbard (Milley's younger sister).

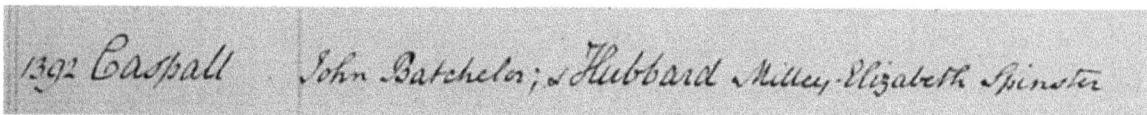

Figure 6: 1805 Marriage

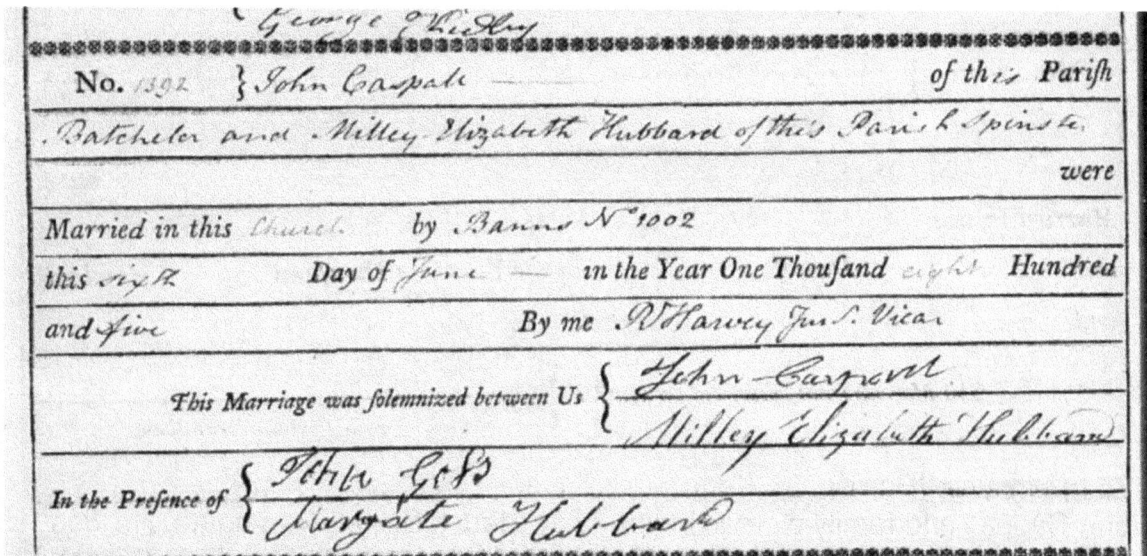

Figure 7: 1805 Banns of Marriage

In 1830 John Caspall, shipright living in Ramsgate was taxed. He is recorded in the Dover Poll books.

Figure 8: 1830. UK Poll Books & Electoral Registers

Milley and the children George and Margaret are found in the 1841 census for Ramsgate on Frederick Street (no house number given). She is listed as a dressmaker. I do not know where John was in this year but suspect he was working on a ship somewhere.

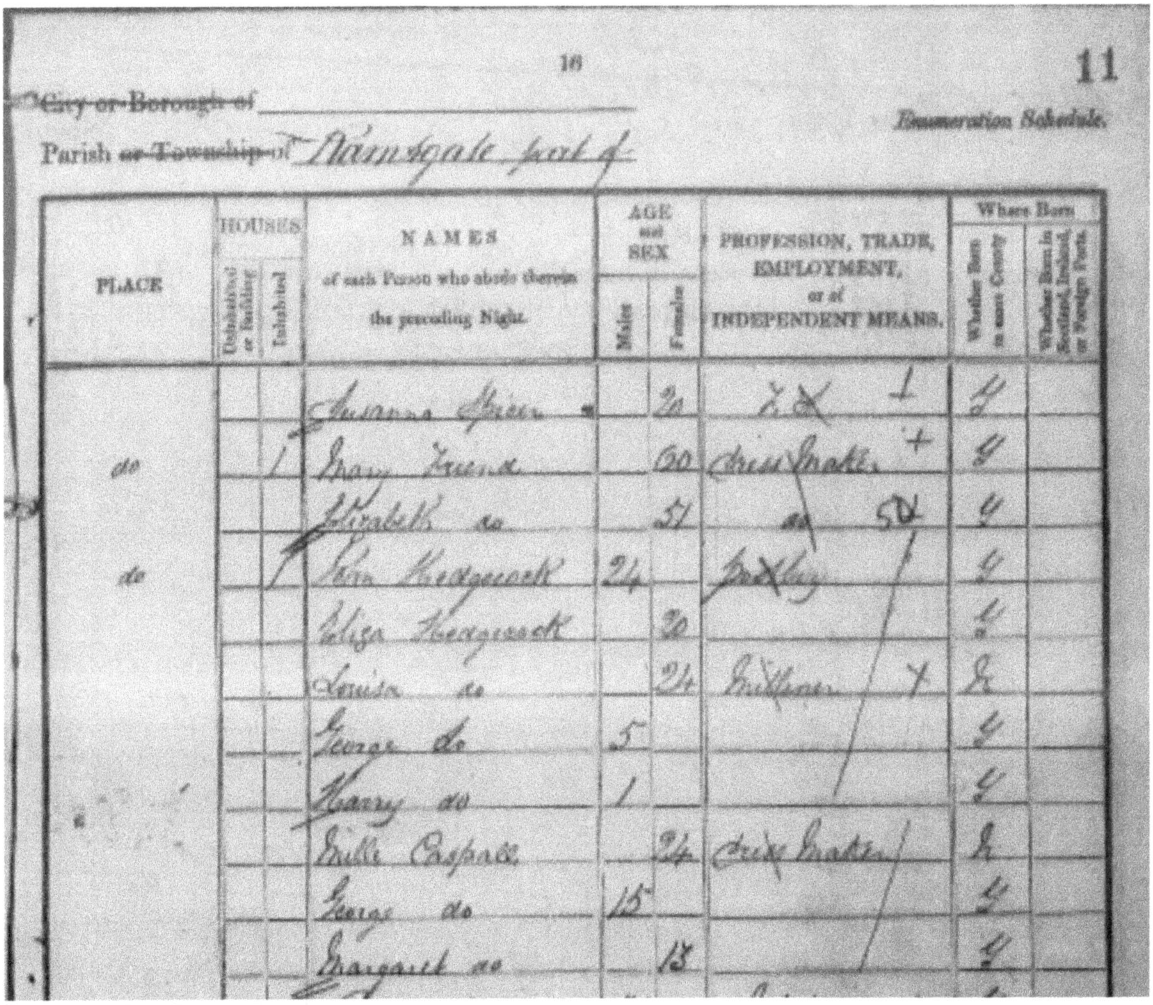

Figure 9: 1841 Census Ramsgate

1851 Census of Ramsgate, Kent:
John Caspall and family were living at 22 Frederick Street, Ramsgate. He was shown as a Shipwright aged 73 and born in Folkestone. His wife Milley Elizabeth aged 67, their daughter Margaret aged 21 and grand-daughter Laura aged 5. Frederick Street is no longer on the modern map but I believe it to have been close to Waterloo street, Brunswick Street. This area was possibly the early Ramsgate.

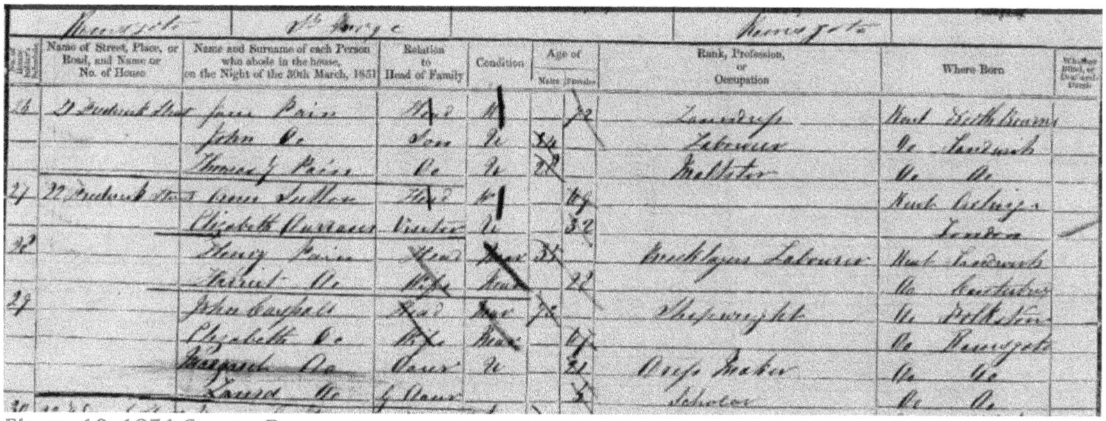

Figure 10: 1851 Census Ramsgate

John died not long after the 1851 census was taken.

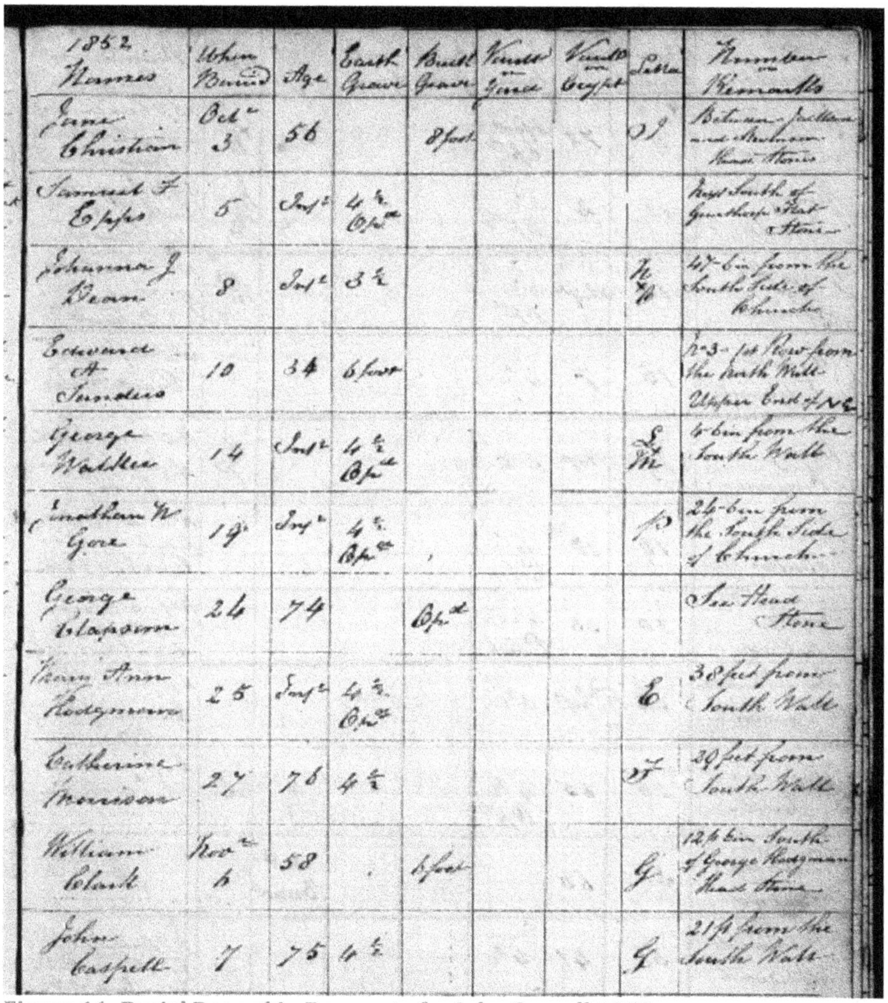

Figure 11: Burial Record in Ramsgate for John Caspall 1852

His Death Certificate shows John Caspall as having been a Shipwright by occupation and he was 75 years of age at the time of his death from natural decay. The death occurred at Frederick Street, Ramsgate on the 31st October 1852 and a Dorothy Dowell was present at the time of his death. Her address is shown as 10 St. Vincent Place, Ramsgate.

1861 Census Ramsgate Kent
Charles Caspall 1848 Ramsgate, Kent, England Grandson
Margaret Caspall 1831 Ramsgate, Kent, England Daughter
Milley E Caspall 1787 Ramsgate, Kent, England Head

Milley Elizabeth died in the June quarter of 1871, she was 83 years old.

Family Group Sheet for John Caspall

Husband:		John Caspall
	b:	02 Apr 1780 in Folkestone, Kent Eng
	m:	06 Jun 1805 in St. Laurence, Ramsgate, Kent Eng.
	d:	31 Oct 1852 in Ramsgate, Kent Eng
	Father:	James Caspall
	Mother:	Sarah Peerless
Wife:		Milly Elizabeth Hubbard
	b:	27 Jul 1788 in Saint Laurence, Thanet, Kent, Eng
	d:	13 May 1871 in Ramsgate, Kent Eng
	Father:	Philip Hubbard
	Mother:	Elizabeth (Betsy) Moses Hinds
Children:		
1	Name:	James Goss Caspall
M	b:	15 Apr 1806 in Saint Laurence, Thanet, Kent, Eng
	m:	18 Sep 1830 in Stoke Damerel, Devon Eng
	Spouse:	Caroline Littlejohns
2	Name:	Sarah Ann Caspall
F	b:	04 Sep 1808 in St. Laurence, Thanet Kent
3	Name:	Milly Elizabeth Caspall
F	b:	04 Sep 1808 in St. Laurence, Thanet Kent
4	Name:	Mary Ann Caspall
F	b:	29 Jun 1817 in St. Laurence, Thanet Kent
5	Name:	John Henry Caspall
M	b:	14 Nov 1819 in St. Lawrence, Ramsgate, Kent Eng
	m:	27 Oct 1839 in Ebenezer Chapel, Ramsgate Kent Eng.
	d:	12 Mar 1902 in Thanet, Kent
	Spouse:	Mary Laming
6	Name:	Frances Caspall
F	b:	14 Oct 1821 in St. Laurence, Thanet Kent
7	Name:	George Caspall
M	b:	14 Mar 1824 in St. Laurence, Thanet Kent
8	Name:	Margaret Caspall
F	b:	15 Jan 1826 in St. Laurence, Thanet Kent

John Caspall 1819-1902

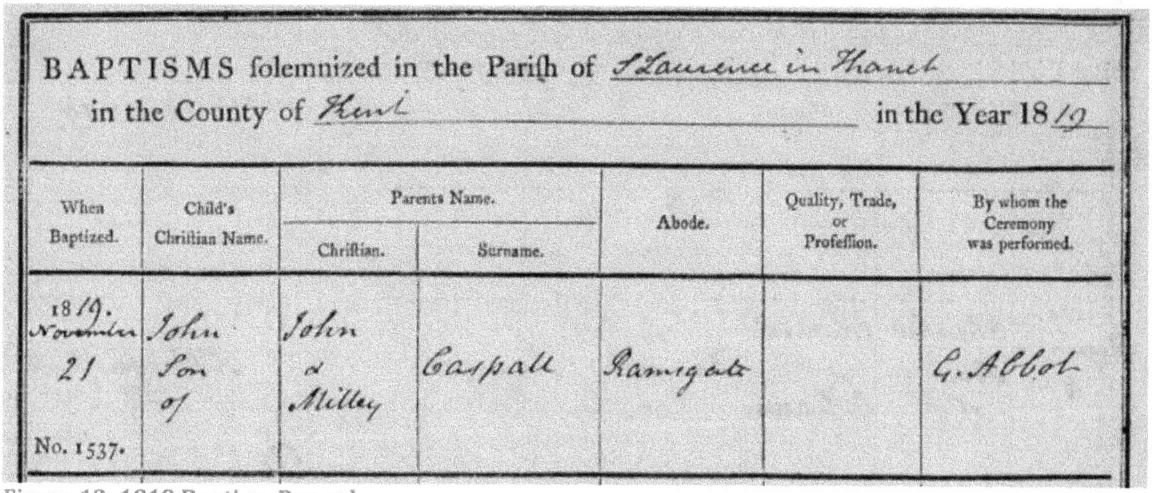

Figure 12: 1819 Baptism Record

John Henry Caspall was baptised in Ramsgate on 21 November 1819 to John and Milly Caspall.

Marriage: John CASPAL [sic] married Mary LAMING on 27 Oct. 1839 in Ebenezer Chapel, Ramsgate, Kent. John was of full age (over 21) a bachelor and shipwright. He was the son of John CASPALL also a shipwright and living at Garden Row, Ramsgate. Mary was of full age, a spinster and the daughter of Henry LAMING, a seaman. She lived 16 York Street, Ramsgate. Witnesses were Richard HAWKINS and Henry PETTMAN.

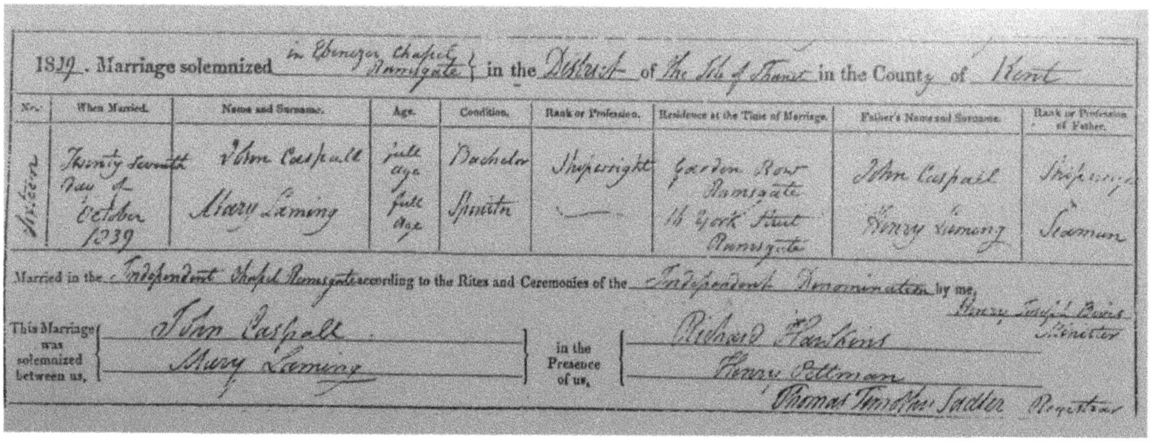

Further research shows that Mary Laming's mother was Mary Smith.

<u>1841 Census Lewisham Kent Loam Pit Hill</u>
John Caspell 25 Kent, England   labourer
Mary Caspell 25 Kent, England

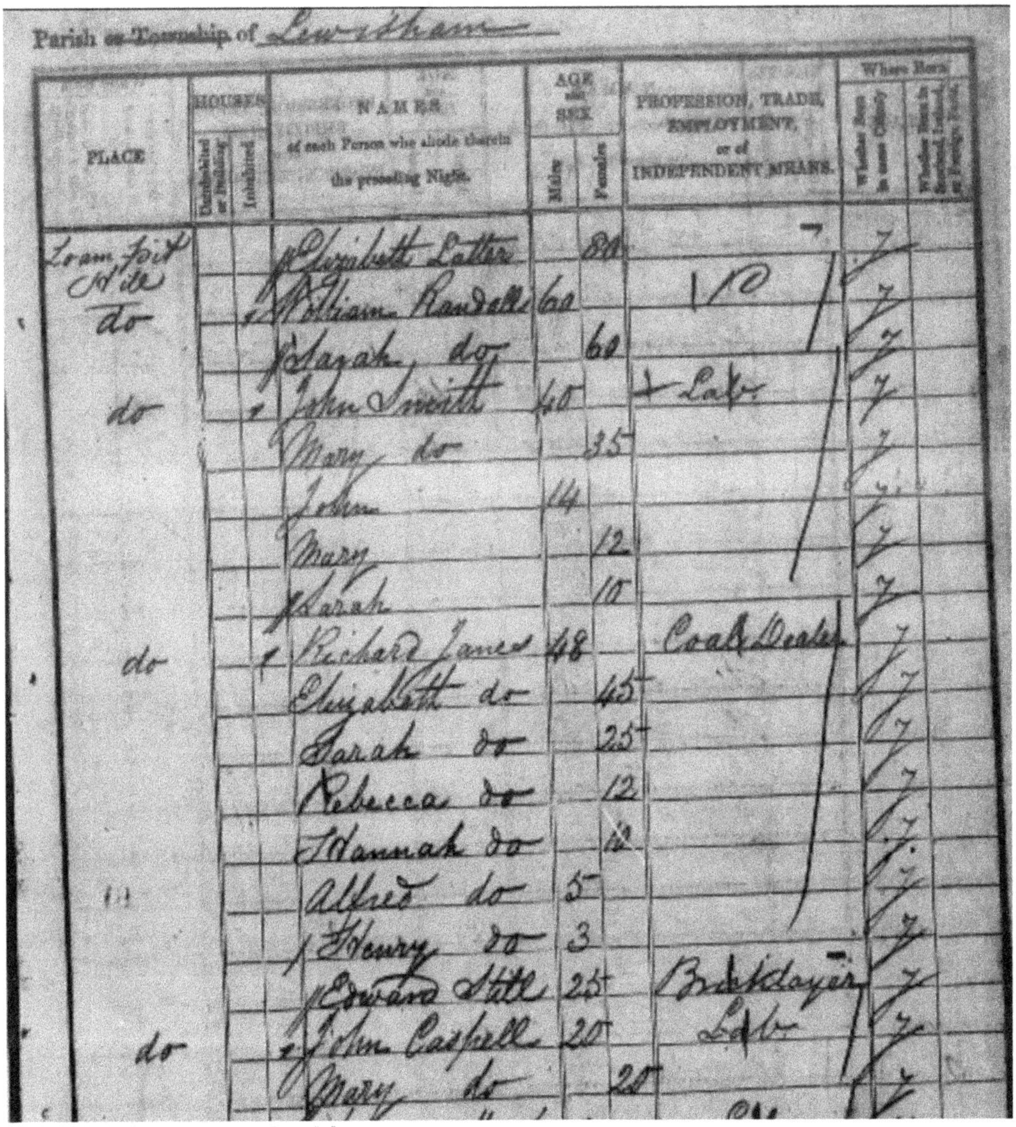

Parish or Township of Lewisham

PLACE	HOUSES: Uninhabited or Building	HOUSES: Inhabited	NAMES of each Person who abode therein the preceding Night.	AGE and SEX: Males	AGE and SEX: Females	PROFESSION, TRADE, EMPLOYMENT, or of INDEPENDENT MEANS.	Where Born: Whether Born in same County	Where Born: Whether Born in Scotland, Ireland, or Foreign Parts
Loam Pit Hill			Elizabeth Latter		80		y	
do		1	William Randall	60		I S	y	
			Sarah do		60		y	
do		1	John Smith	40		Lab	y	
			Mary do		35		y	
			John	14			y	
			Mary		12		y	
			Sarah		10		y	
do		1	Richard James	48		Coal Dealer	y	
			Elizabeth do		45		y	
			Sarah do		25		y	
			Rebecca do		12		y	
			Hannah do		12		y	
			Alfred do	5			y	
			Henry do	3			y	
			Edward Stile	25		Bricklayer	y	
do		1	John Caspell	20		Lab	y	
			Mary do		20		y	

Figure 13: 1841 Census Lewisham

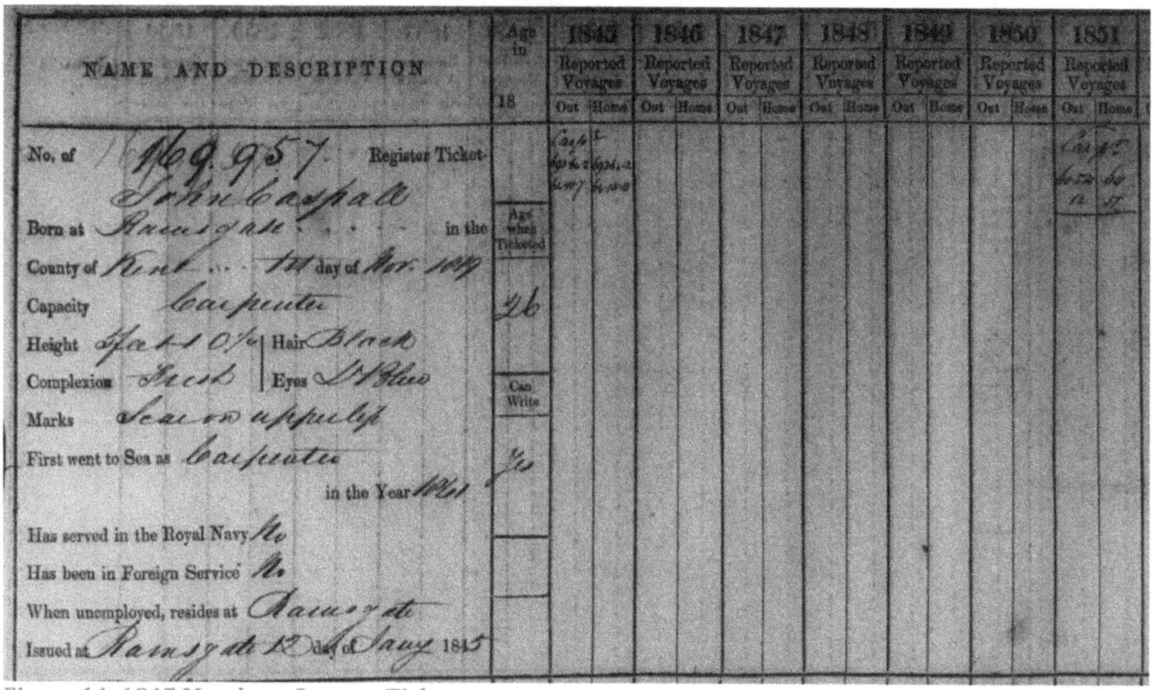
NAME AND DESCRIPTION

No. of 469.957 Register Ticket

John Caspall

Born at Ramsgate in the County of Kent 1st day of Nov. 1819

Capacity Carpenter

Height 5 ft 0½ Hair Black

Complexion Fresh Eyes Lt Blue

Marks Scar on upper lip

First went to Sea as Carpenter in the Year 1841

Has served in the Royal Navy No

Has been in Foreign Service No

When unemployed, resides at Ramsgate

Issued at Ramsgate 12 day of Jany 1845

Age in 18 | Age when Ticketed 26 | Can Write Yes

1845 1846 1847 1848 1849 1850 1851 — Reported Voyages — Out Home

Figure 14: 1845 Merchant Seaman Ticket

<u>Kentish Gazette - Tuesday 07 September 1847</u>: Thanet Horticultural & Floricultural Society. Cottager's Prizes: John Caspall - 6 best pears, 8 kidney potatoes, 3rd best round kidney potatoes,

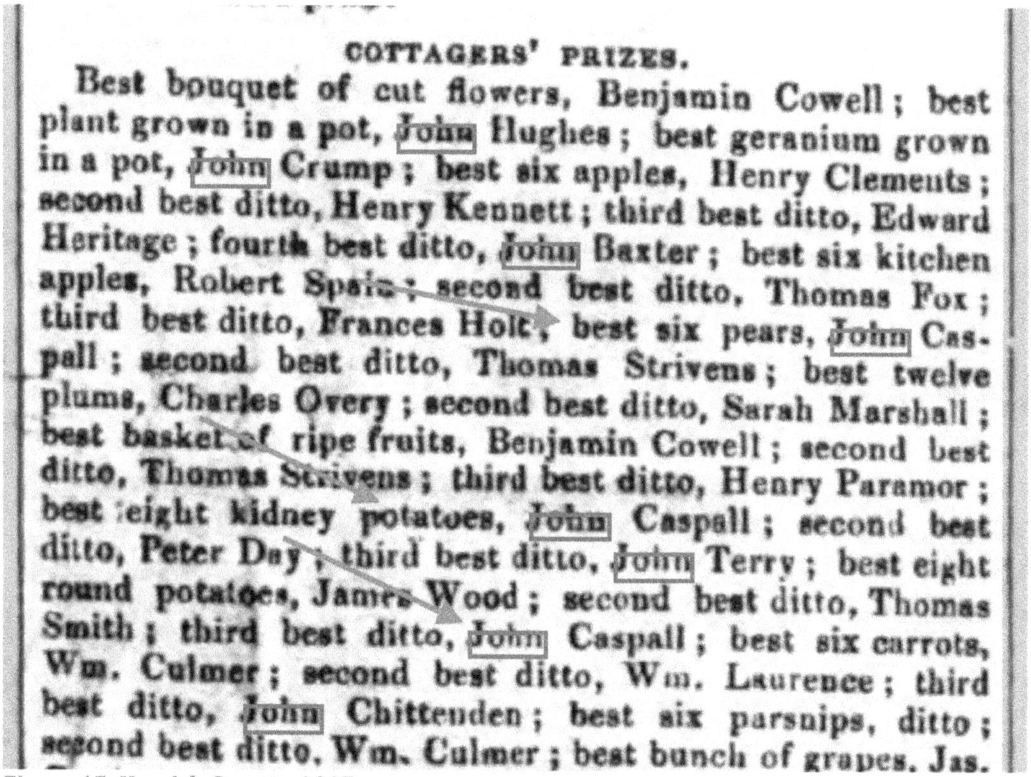
COTTAGERS' PRIZES.

Best bouquet of cut flowers, Benjamin Cowell; best plant grown in a pot, John Hughes; best geranium grown in a pot, John Crump; best six apples, Henry Clements; second best ditto, Henry Kennett; third best ditto, Edward Heritage; fourth best ditto, John Baxter; best six kitchen apples, Robert Spain; second best ditto, Thomas Fox; third best ditto, Frances Holt; best six pears, John Caspall; second best ditto, Thomas Strivens; best twelve plums, Charles Overy; second best ditto, Sarah Marshall; best basket of ripe fruits, Benjamin Cowell; second best ditto, Thomas Strivens; third best ditto, Henry Paramor; best eight kidney potatoes, John Caspall; second best ditto, Peter Day; third best ditto, John Terry; best eight round potatoes, James Wood; second best ditto, Thomas Smith; third best ditto, John Caspall; best six carrots, Wm. Culmer; second best ditto, Wm. Laurence; third best ditto, John Chittenden; best six parsnips, ditto; second best ditto, Wm. Culmer; best bunch of grapes, Jas.

Figure 15: Kentish Gazette 1847

<u>1851 census Ramsgate Kent: 11 Leopold Place</u>

John CASPAL, head, married, 31, shipwright, born Ramsgate Kent
Mary, wife, married, 32, born Ramsgate, Kent
Amelia E., dau, 8 born Ramsgate Kent
Jane H., dau, 6, born Ramsgate Kent
John, son, 4, born Ramsgate Kent
Charles W., son, 2, born Ramsgate Kent
Ellen M., dau, 3 months, born Ramsgate Kent

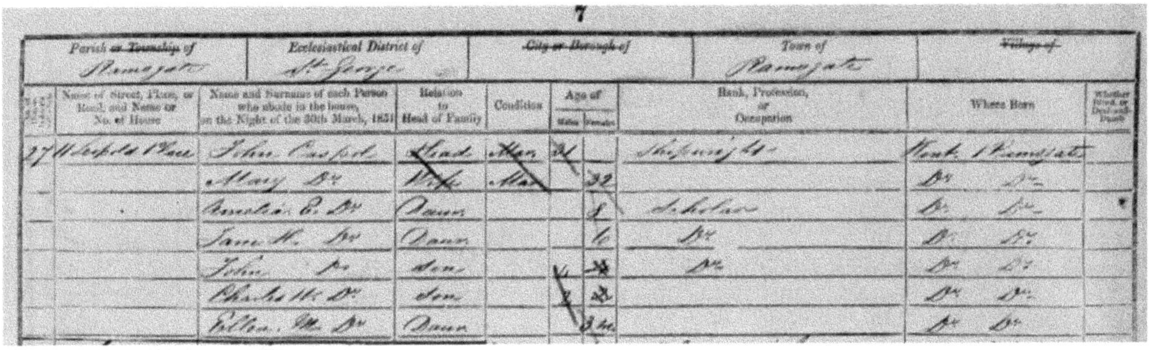
7

Parish or Township of: Ramsgate	Ecclesiastical District of: St George	City or Borough of	Town of: Ramsgate	Village of

No. of Householder's Schedule	Name of Street, Place, or Road, and Name or No. of House	Name and Surname of each Person who abode in the house, on the Night of the 30th March, 1851	Relation to Head of Family	Condition	Age of Males	Age of Females	Rank, Profession, or Occupation	Where Born
27	Leopold Place	John Caspal	Head	Mar	31		Shipwright	Kent Ramsgate
		Mary Do	Wife	Mar		32		Do Do
		Amelia E. Do	Daur			8	Scholar	Do Do
		Jane H. Do	Daur			6	Do	Do Do
		John Do	Son		4		Do	Do Do
		Charles W. Do	Son		2			Do Do
		Ellen M. Do	Daur			3 m		Do Do

Figure 16: 1851 Census Ramsgate

Thomas Vantier surrendered to answer a charge of having, on the 24th ult., assaulted John Caspell. It appears that both parties are shipwrights, employed by different masters. On Sunday afternoon, about half-past 3 o'clock, complainant was in the pier-yard, when the defendant came up to him, and after using some foul language towards him, struck him on the chest two or three times. In proof of this, complainant called his sister and another female to whom he was talking at the time defendant came up. Defendant said that as he was passing the complainant he said "There goes one of them —— foreigners who is eating my bread." He then stepped up to him, and said if he was a better man than he was he had better try it, but he did not hit him. Defendant's wife, who was in front of him the whole time, swore that there was no blow struck, and in this she was corroborated by another witness. The Bench dismissed the case, and ordered the complainant to pay the costs, 13s. 6d.

Tuesday 04 March 1856, South Eastern Gazette, Kent, England

Mary (Laming) Caspall was buried in Ramsgate on 24 August 1856.

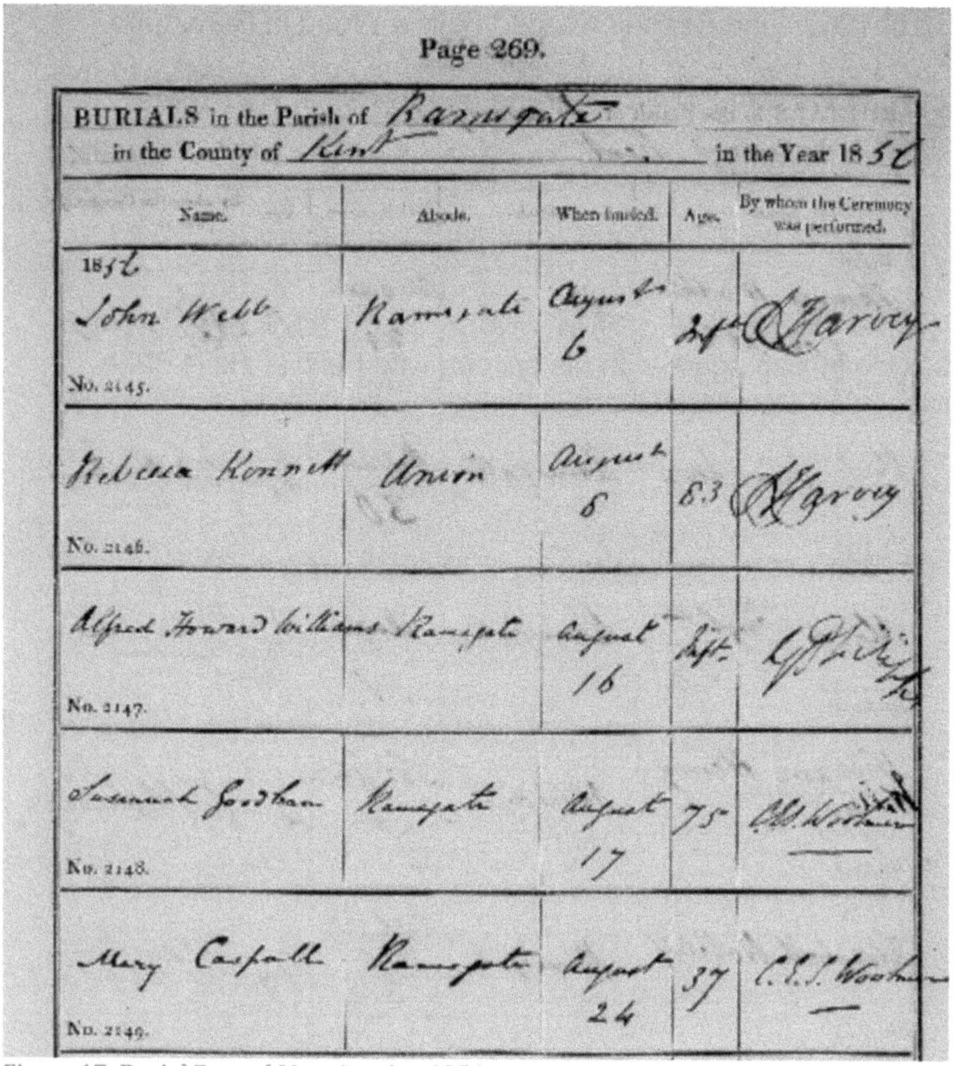
Page 269.

BURIALS in the Parish of Ramsgate in the County of Kent in the Year 1856

Name.	Abode.	When buried.	Age.	By whom the Ceremony was performed.
1856 John Webb No. 2145.	Ramsgate	August 6	24	[illegible] Harvey
Rebecca Kennett No. 2146.	Union	August 8	83	[illegible] Harvey
Alfred Howard Williams No. 2147.	Ramsgate	August 16	4	[illegible]
Susannah Goodham No. 2148.	Ramsgate	August 17	75	[illegible]
Mary Caspall No. 2149.	Ramsgate	August 24	37	C. E. S. Woodham

Figure 17: Burial Record Mary Laming 1856

Erridge v. Meagher.—A claim of £2 19s. 11d. for work done, money lent, and refreshment. All the parties at the time resided at Ramsgate, where, in the winter of 1855-56, defendant and a man named Caspall had engaged to break up a wrecked ship at that port for a stipulated sum. They employed plaintiff and others in the work; but Erridge failed to get the wages due to him, and forming part of the present claim. His Honour observed that Caspall should have been included in the summons, but still though in joint concern, each party was liable. He should make an order for Meagher to pay, and he must sue Caspall for the half of what they were jointly liable.

Kentish Gazette - Tuesday 15 December 1857 Court Case re ship and wages not paid

In the 4th quarter of 1860 John Caspall married Felicia Wood in Ramsgate.

In 1861 John and second wife Felicia are living on King St. in Ramsgate

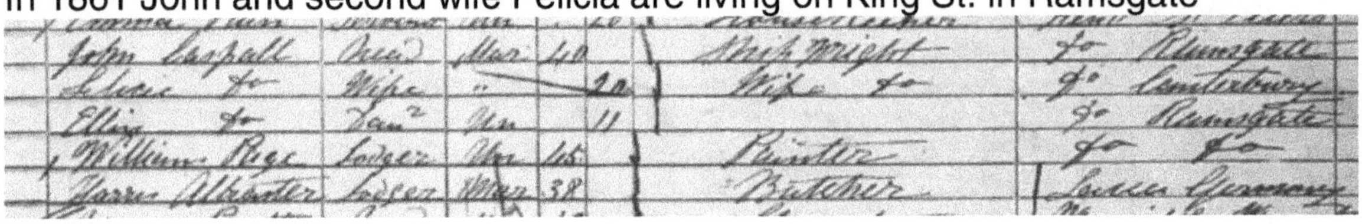

John Caspall	Head	Mar	40	Shipwright	Do Ramsgate
Felicia do	Wife	"	20	Wife do	Do Canterbury
Ellis do	Dau	Un	11		Do Ramsgate
William Rice	Lodger	Un	15	Printer	Do do
James Alkhater	Lodger	Mar	38	Butcher	Saxe Germany

Figure 18: 1861 Census Ramsgate

In 1871 John is living in Ramsgate with his second wife Felicia. He is 52, a shipright and living at 51 Denmark Road.

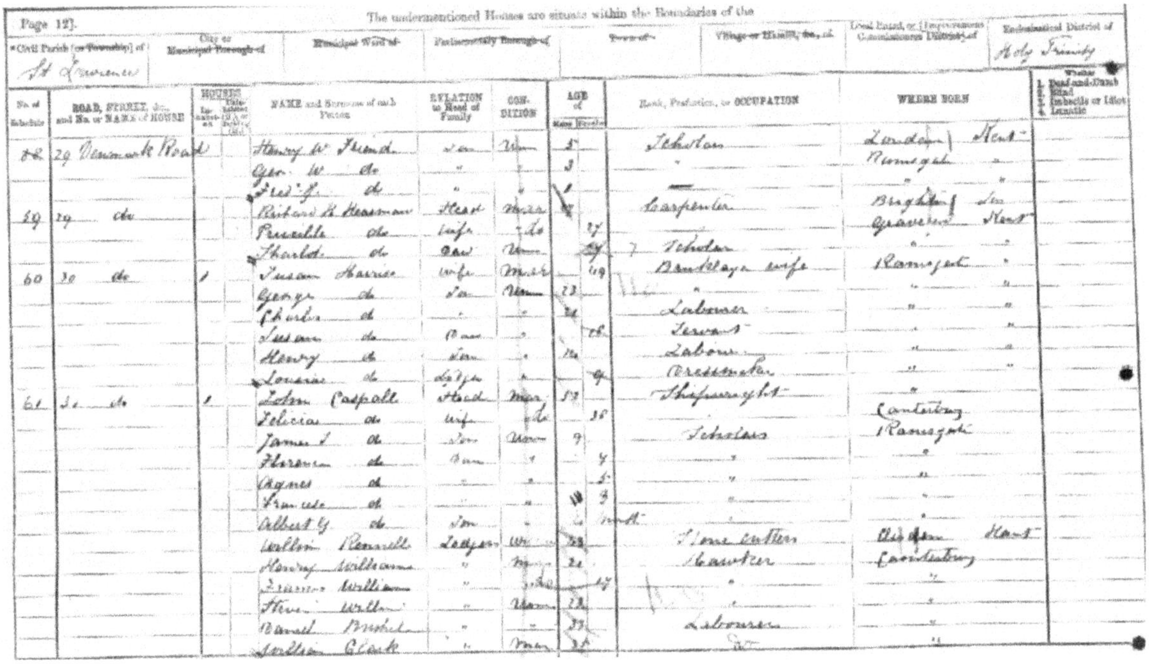

Page 12] The undermentioned Houses are situate within the Boundaries of the

Civil Parish [or Township] of St Lawrence — Ecclesiastical District of Holy Trinity

No. of Schedule	Road, Street, &c., and No. or Name of House	Houses	Name and Surname of each Person	Relation to Head of Family	Condition	Age Males	Age Females	Rank, Profession, or Occupation	Where Born
58	29 Denmark Road		Henry W. Friend	Son	Un	5		Scholar	London Kent
			Geo. W. do	"		3			Ramsgate
			Fred. J. do	"		1			"
59	29 do		Richard R. Heasman	Head	Mar			Carpenter	Brighton Sussex
			Priscilla do	Wife	do		37		Gravesend Kent
			Charlotte do	Dau	Un		7	Scholar	Ramsgate
60	30 do	1	Susan Harris	Wife	Mar		49	Bankleyer wife	"
			George do	Son	Un	23		Labourer	"
			Charles do			21			"
			Susan do	Dau			18	Servant	"
			Henry do	Son		16		Labourer	"
			Louisa do	Lodger			9	Dressmaker	"
61	31 do	1	John Caspall	Head	Mar	52		Shipwright	
			Felicia do	Wife	do		35		Canterbury
			James do	Son	Un	9		Scholar	Ramsgate
			Florence do	Dau			7		"
			Agnes do				5		"
			Frances do				3		"
			Albert G. do	Son					"
			William Rennell	Lodger	Un	23		Stone cutter	Aldershot Hants
			Henry Williams	"	Mar	21		Hawker	Canterbury
			Frances Williams	"			17		"
			Stephen Williams	"	Un	18			"
			Daniel Mitchell	"		33		Labourer	"
			William Clark	"	Mar	35		do	"

Figure 19: 1871 Census Ramsgate

1881 Census shows 61 year John, a shipright, is living with second wife Felicia at 1 Rural Cottages, Ramsgate

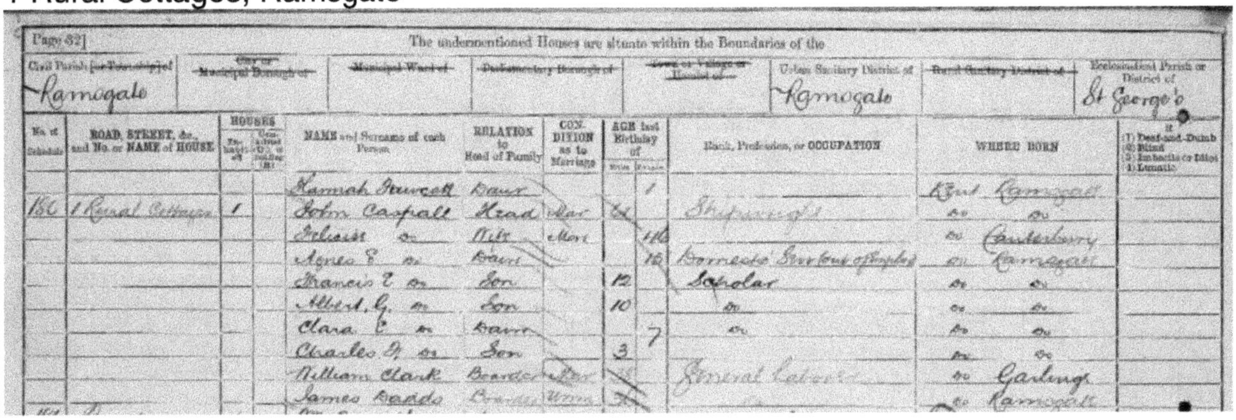

Page 32] The undermentioned Houses are situate within the Boundaries of the

Civil Parish of Ramsgate — Urban Sanitary District of Ramsgate — Ecclesiastical Parish or District of St George's

No. of Schedule	Road, Street, &c., and No. or Name of House	Houses Inhabited	Name and Surname of each Person	Relation to Head of Family	Condition as to Marriage	Age Males	Age Females	Rank, Profession, or Occupation	Where Born
			Hannah Fawcett	Daur			7		Kent Ramsgate
180	1 Rural Cottages	1	John Caspall	Head	Mar	61		Shipwright	do do
			Felicia do	Wife	Mar		46		do Canterbury
			Agnes E do	Daur			16	Domestic Servant out of employ	do Ramsgate
			Francis E do	Son		12		Scholar	do do
			Albert G. do	Son		10		do	do do
			Clara E do	Daur			7	do	do do
			Charles G do	Son		3			do do
			William Clark	Boarder	Wid			General Labourer	do Garlinge
			James Dadds	Boarder	Unm				do Ramsgate

Figure 20: 1881 Census Ramsgate

1891 finds John and Felicia still in Ramsgate at 1 Rural Cottages.

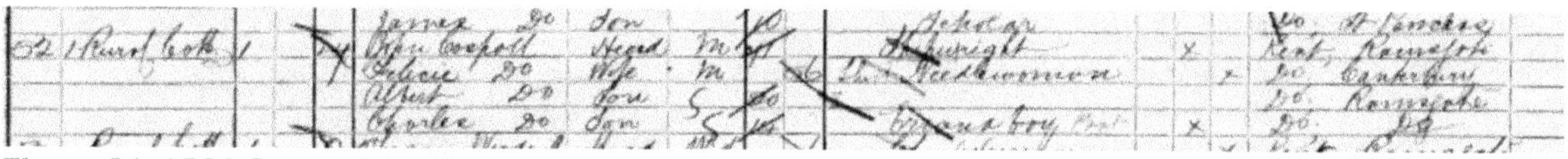

			James Do	Son		10	Scholar		Do. St Pancras
52	1 Rural Cott	1	John Caspall	Head	M		Shipwright	X	Kent, Ramsgate
			Felice Do	Wife	M		Needlewoman	X	Do Canterbury
			Albert Do	Son	S	20			Do. Ramsgate
			Charles Do	Son	S	16	Errand boy	X	Do. Do

Figure 21: 1891 Census Ramsgate

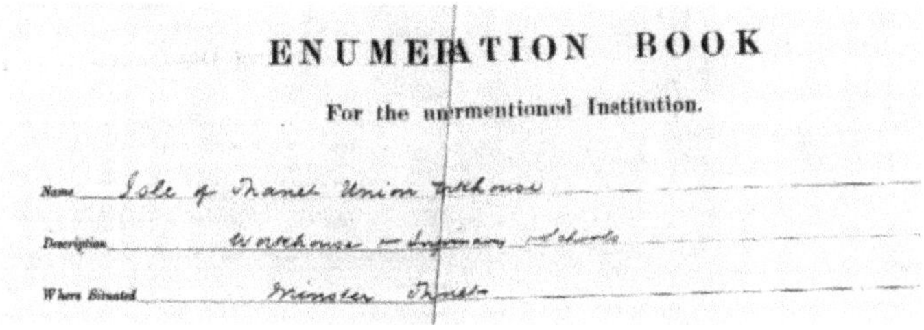

ENUMERATION BOOK

For the undermentioned Institution.

Name: Isle of Thanet Union Workhouse

Description: Workhouse – Infirmary – Schools

Where Situated: Minster Thanet

In 1901 John is an inmate in the Isle of Thanet Union Workhouse . He is listed as an 80 year old widower from Ramsgate. This census was taken on 27 April 1901.

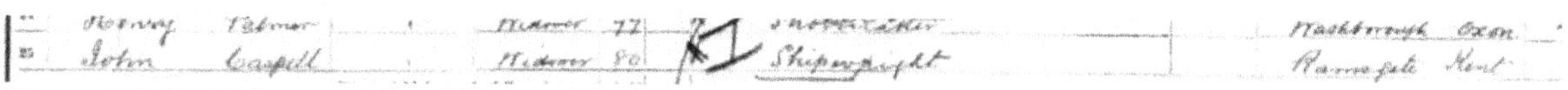

	Harvey Palmer	Widower 77		Shoemaker	Marlborough Oxon
25	John Caspell	Widower 80		Shipwright	Ramsgate Kent

Figure 22: 1901 Census Isle of Thanet Workhouse

John died at the age of 81 in March 1902 still In the Thanet Workhouse.

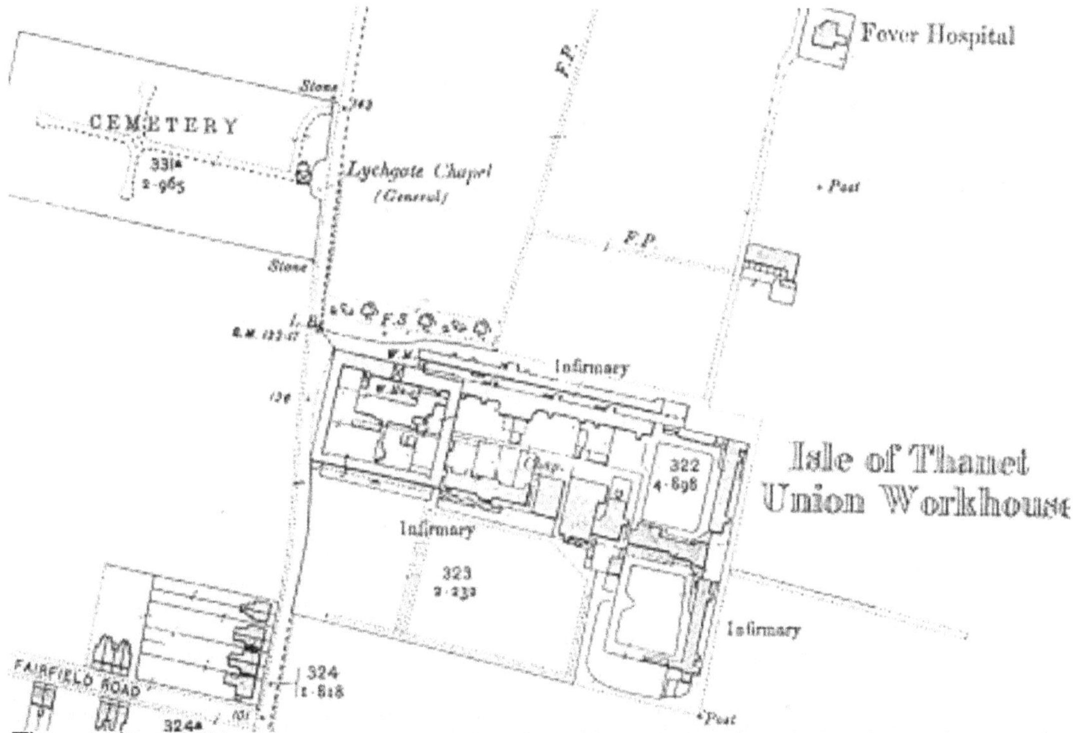

Thanet site, 1907.

Figure 23: Isle of Thanet Workhouse, ca early 1900s

His death notice appeared inThe Thanet Advertiser March 15, 1902 under Deaths

DEATHS.

London—March 4, at the Great Northern Hospital, Richard Foster Moys, of Ramsgate, aged 46.

Ramsgate—March 9, at 1, Vincent Villas, Crescent-road. Emma Wright, aged 57.

Ramsgate—March 10, Thomas Ernest Boyd Broadbent, aged 49.

Ramsgate—March 11, Frances Ofield, aged 73.

Ramsgate—March 12, at 13, Cross-street, John Caspall, aged 83.

Figure 24: John Caspall ca 1890s with his grandchildren Lillian & Charles

John Henry Caspall 1847-1885

John Henry Caspall, my great-great grandfather, was baptised in Ramsgate on 30 April 1847 to parents John Henry Caspall Sr. and Mary Laming.

Birth: Registered by mother Mary (Laming) Caspall on 15 May 1847 as being born Rose Cottage, Ramsgate Kent. Father shown as John Caspall, shipwright. Registered Ramsgate, Isle of Thanet, Kent

In 1861 we find John Henry on board the ship Rye Merchant
Name: John Caspall. Age: 16, Cabin Boy
Civil parish: Vessels. Town: Off Haisborough. County/Island: Misc Ships at Sea or Abroad. Country: England
Source information: RG9/4456. Registration district: Misc Ships. ED, institution, or vessel: Rye Merchant. Folio: 12. GSU Number: 543288

Thomas Beer 1844 Margate, Kent, England A B Seaman
John Bushell 1797 Margate, Kent, England Master
John Caspall 1845 Ramsgate, Kent, England Cabin Boy
Bengaman Cowell 1825 Ramsgate, Kent, England A B Seaman
John Waring 1844 Folkestone, Kent, England A B Seaman
John Williams 1839 Ramsgate, Kent, England Mate

(Form A.)

CENSUS
OF
THE POPULATION,
1861.

FORM FOR VESSELS.

PREPARED UNDER THE DIRECTION OF ONE OF HER
MAJESTY'S PRINCIPAL SECRETARIES OF STATE.

NAME OF VESSEL.	*Rye Merchant*
Port or Place to which she belongs	*Ramsgate*
Her Tonnage	*9 t*
Her Description, and the Trade in which she is employed	*in the costing trade*
Name of Master	*John Bushell*

Place at which the Schedule is delivered to the Master
and the Date of Delivery.

Seaham April 1 /1861

Position of the Vessel at Midnight, April 7th, 1861.

Hailing on the Share Lights bearing S. W.
distance 5 Miles

On 03 Mar 1868 he married Mary Ann Williams in St. George's Church in Ramsgate. He was 22 years old and his father was recorded as John Henry Caspall, shipright. She was 20 and recorded as the daughter of William Henry Williams and he was listed as a Mariner.

Figure 25: 1868 Marriage

1871 England Census > Kent > Vessels > District Cambria on vessel "Cambria" with total 6 crew members:
#3 John Henry Caspall, married, 25, man, b Ramsgate Kent

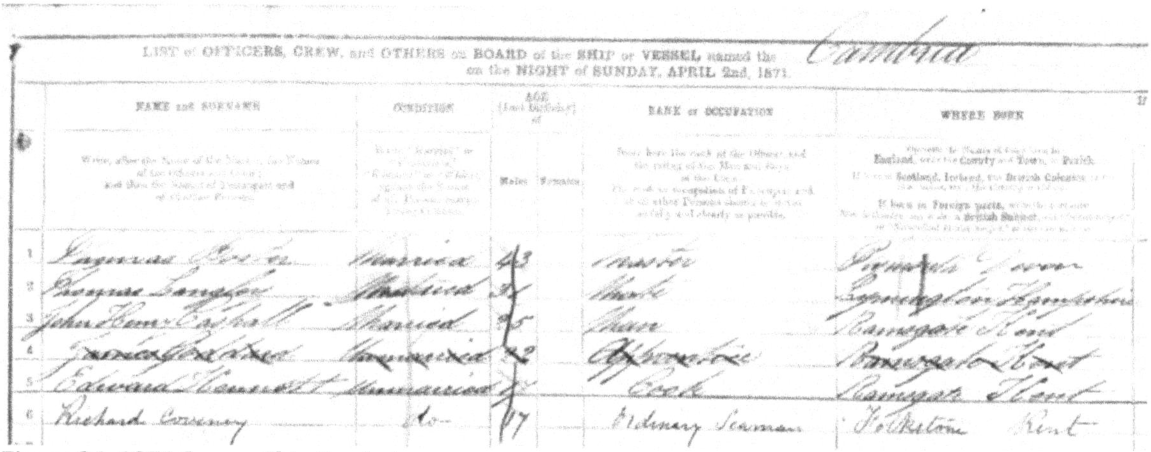

Figure 26: 1871 Census Ship Cambria

1881 census on vessel "William"

Census Place:Ramsgate, Kent, England
Source:FHL Film 1341236   PRO Ref RG11   Piece 0992   Folio 72 Page
John Henry CASPALL M 27 M Ramsgate, Kent Occ:Master
Robert S. DAWSON U 22 M Ramsgate, Kent Occ:Second Hand
William WALKER M 29 M Dudley, Stafford Occ:Third Hand
Patrick KELLEY U 20 M Galway, Ireland Occ:Fourth Hand
Thomas HARRIS U 13 M Whitstable, Kent Occ:Cook
Frederick BRIGHT U 13 M Whitstable, Kent Occ:Passenger

John was the Ship Master and you can see that he signed the Census form
personally.

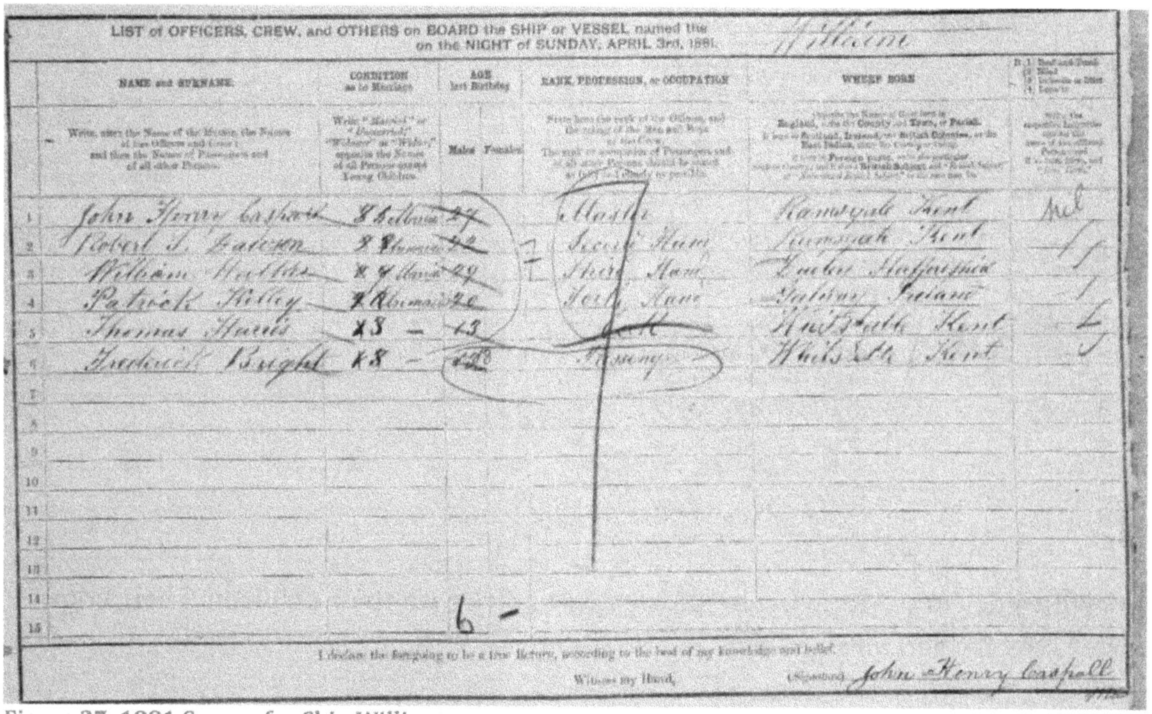

Figure 27: 1881 Census for Ship William

CENSUS

or

THE POPULATION,

1881.

SCHEDULE FOR VESSELS.

PREPARED UNDER THE DIRECTION OF THE LOCAL
GOVERNMENT BOARD,
PURSUANT TO THE ACT OF 43 & 44 VICT., c. 37.

NAME of VESSEL	*William*
Official Number (if any)	*43579*
PORT of Place to which she belongs	*Ramsgate*
Her Tonnage	*37. 98*
Her DESCRIPTION, and the Trade in which she is employed	*Ketch Fishing*
NAME of MASTER	*J. H. Caspall*

Place at which the Schedule is delivered to the
Master, and the Date of Delivery.

Yarmouth March 28th 1881

Position of the Vessel at Midnight, April 3rd, 1881.

At Sea

His wife Mary Ann was living in Ramsgate in 1881 with their children. Their home was 3 May's Villas, May's Road.

In 1881 John was charged a few times for drunkeness.

DRUNK AND DISORDERLY.

John Caspell. a fisherman, was summoned for being drunk and disorderly in West Cliff-road, on the 27th of April.—Defendant pleaded guilty. —P. C. Macarthy stated that at 7 p.m. on the day in question, he was in West Cliff-road, when he saw the defendant there very drunk and rolling and falling about. Witness took his name and a man then led defendant away.—In answer to the charge, defendant said he had been working night and day, and unfortunately took a little too much. He did not interfere with any one, nor did he fall about.—Fined 1s. and 10s. costs.

Joseph Hewitt was then summoned for being

Saturday 07 May 1881, Thanet Advertiser, Kent, England

John Caspell was charged with being drunk in Crescent-road, on the 13th inst.—P.C. Wells stated that on the day in question, about 11.25 he was on duty in Crescent-road, when he saw defendant quite drunk. He had been drunk the night before.—Defendant said he was not drunk, he was going home to supper, and went to sea about 1 o'clock, so he could not have been very drunk.—The Magistrates dismissed the case.

Saturday 24 September 1881, Thanet Advertiser, Kent, England

In 1882 John was sued in court for not sending one of his children to school and allowing the child to miss over 60 days in three months.

THE ADJOURNED SCHOOL ATTENDANCE CASE.

John Caspell was summoned last week for not sending his child to school.—Mr. Lewis, school attendance officer, said that the child made 32 attendances out of 99 from the 1st March to the 24th of May.—The Clerk said that this case was adjourned last week to enable defendant's wife, who then appeared, to bring witnesses to prove that she had taken the child to school on the day named in the summons.—Defendant's wife now said she had not brought any witnesses, as she was away on the day in question, and could not tell whether the child was at school or not.—Fined 6d. and 4s. 6d. costs.

John's death occurred in hospital in Torquay Devon on January 16, 1885 from an accident.

TORQUAY.

FATAL ACCIDENT.—An inquest was held at the Town Hall on Saturday on the body of John Caspell, a seaman on board the Thursby, lying in Torquay harbour. On Tuesday evening last the deceased accidentally fell down the hold of the vessel, and was removed to the Torbay Hospital, where he died of the injuries on Friday evening. The jury returned a verdict of "Accidental death."

Monday 19 January 1885, Western Times, Devon, England

prosecutes, and Mr. W. Earl defends in this case.

John Caspell, a seaman, died in the Torbay Hospital, Torquay, yesterday morning, from the effects of severe injuries sustained through falling into the hold of the collier Thursby, on Tuesday evening, whilst assisting in fastening down the hatches after the discharge of the cargo.

The Methodist Times remarks :—There is at least

Saturday 17 January 1885, Western Morning News, Devon, England

In the 1891 census of Ramsgate Mary Ann is listed as a widow living at 1 Devonshire Terrace. She was misindexed as "Coopell" making finding her a challenge! Her widowed father is living with her. He is recorded as the Organ Cleaner at Christ Church in Ramsgate, and Mary Ann is listed as a Laundress. There are several boarders living with the family, no doubt to help bring in money for Mary Ann to support her young children.

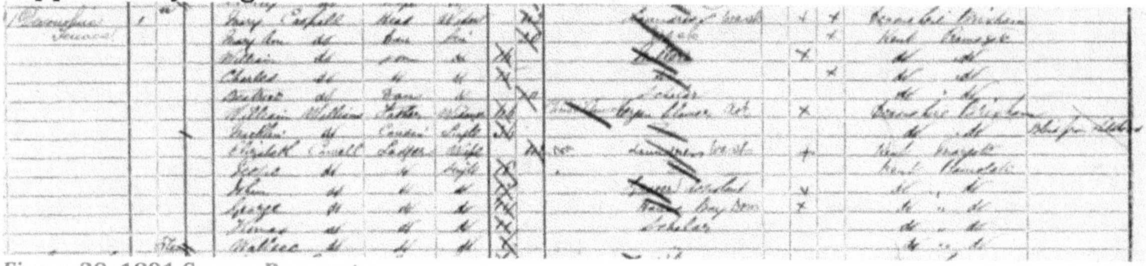

Figure 28: 1891 Census Ramsgate

1901 finds Mary Ann and her father still living together in Ramsgate at 20 Cumberland Road. Mary Ann is a widowed Laundress age 52. Her father is a 77 year old widower, and recorded as working as a wood chopper. Her daughter Beatrice Appleton is living with them.

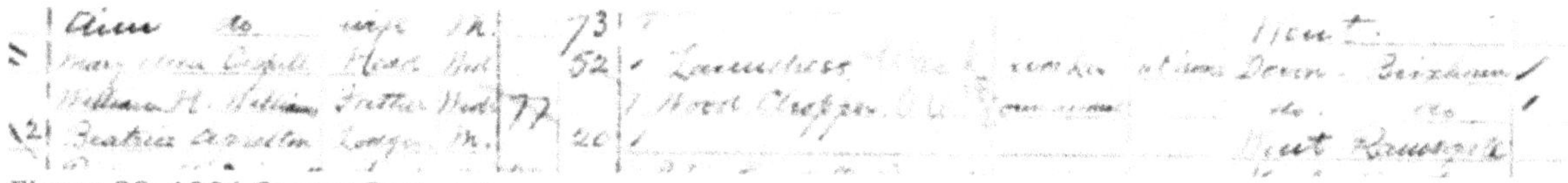

Figure 29: 1901 Census Ramsgate

In 1911 62 year old Mary Ann has moved in with her daughter Beatrice (now married to Charles Britton) and is living in a 9-room house at 7 Liverpool Lawn, Ramsgate.

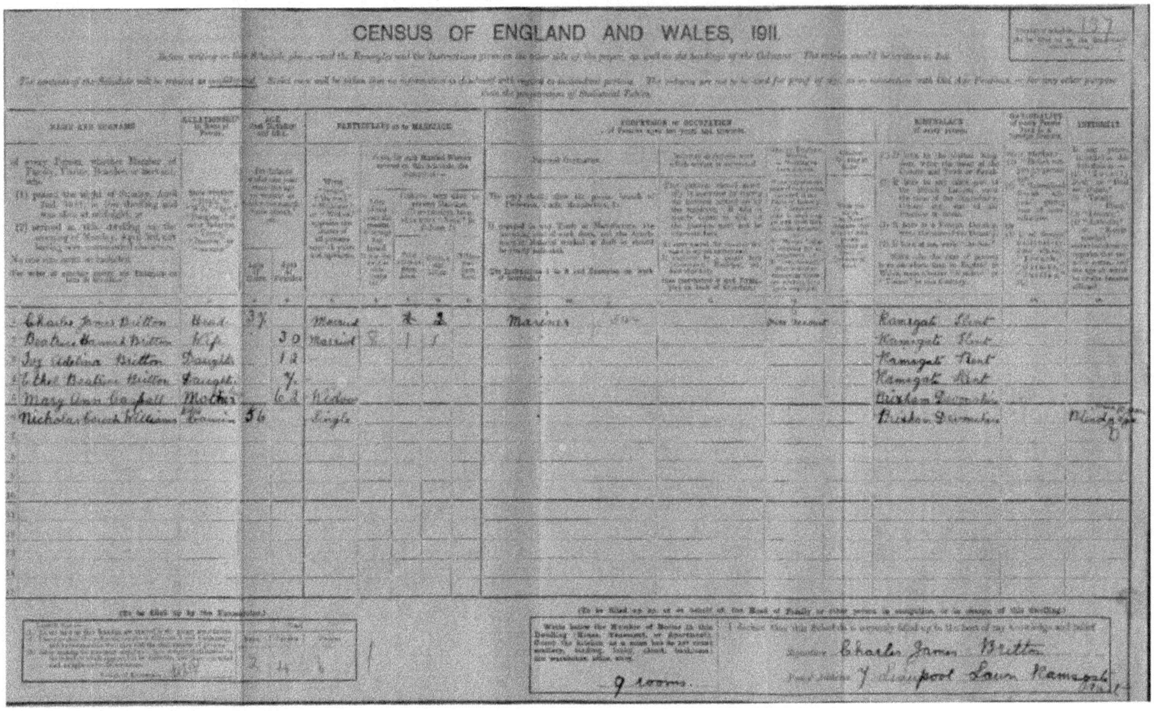

CENSUS OF ENGLAND AND WALES, 1911.

Name and Surname	Relationship to Head of Family	Age (Males)	Age (Females)	Particulars as to Marriage				Profession or Occupation		Birthplace	Infirmity
Charles James Britton	Head	37		Married		[illegible]	2	Mariner	[illegible]	Ramsgate Kent	
Beatrice Hannah Britton	Wife		30	Married	[illegible]	1	1			Ramsgate Kent	
Ivy Adelina Britton	Daughter		12							Ramsgate Kent	
Ethel Beatrice Britton	Daughter		7							Ramsgate Kent	
Mary Ann Caspall	Mother		63	Widow						Brixham Devonshire	
Nicholas Couch Williams	Cousin	56		Single						Brixham Devonshire	Blind [illegible]

9 rooms.

Charles James Britton

7 Liverpool Lawn Ramsgate

Figure 30: 1911 Census Ramsgate

Beatrice's husband Charles Britton is a mariner and Nicholas Couch Williams, a cousin to Beatrice, is listed as being blind since 10 years of age. His age in 1911 is 56. Finding him may help take the Williams family back further than I have taken it (to be discussed later) I have found that his parents were Nicholas and Mary Williams and that he is in several census records with Mary Ann Williams' parents. It seems that Nicholas Williams may be a brother to William Henry Willliams the father of Mary Ann.

Mary Ann died in 1915. Death Certifcate: 14 Aug. 1915, 37 Albert St. Ramsgate. Mary Ann Caspall, female, 67 years, widow of John Henry Caspall a fisherman, died of Chronic Endocarditis for last 8 years. plus nephritis and Synsopsa. M. A. N. Fuller, daughter was present at her death.

Family Group Sheet for John Henry Caspall

Husband:		John Henry Caspall
	b:	30 Apr 1847 in Ramsgate Kent Eng
	m:	03 Mar 1868 in St. George's Parish Church, Ramsgate, Kent Eng
	d:	16 Jan 1895 in Torquay, Devon, England
	Father:	John Henry Caspall
	Mother:	Mary Laming
Wife:		Mary Ann Williams
	b:	12 Aug 1848 in Lower Brixham, Devon Eng
	d:	14 Aug 1915 in Ramsgate, Kent Eng
	Father:	William Henry Williams
	Mother:	Betsey Norman
Children:		
1	Name:	Bepie Caspall
F	b:	Abt. 1869 in Ramsgate, Kent, England
2	Name:	Mary Ann Norman Caspall
F	b:	17 May 1870 in Thanet, Ramsgate, Kent, Eng
	m:	28 Apr 1891 in Christ Church, Ramsgate, Kent Eng
	d:	1955 in England
	Spouse:	Charles Fuller
3	Name:	William Charles Caspall
M	b:	10 Jun 1874 in Ramsgate, Kent Eng
	m:	07 Nov 1893 in Christ Church, Ramsgate, Kent Eng
	d:	30 Nov 1918 in Suffolk, England
	Spouse:	Alice Louisa Castle
4	Name:	Charles W. Caspall
M	b:	1875 in Ramsgate, Kent England
5	Name:	Beatrice Hannah Norman Caspall
F	b:	1881 in Ramsgate, Kent England
	m:	Mar 1901 in Thanet, Kent, England
	Spouse:	Charles Samuel Appelton

My Caspall line daughtered out with the birth of Mary Ann Norman Caspall in 1870. She married Charles Fuller in 1891 and this family will be discussed in the Fuller Family book.

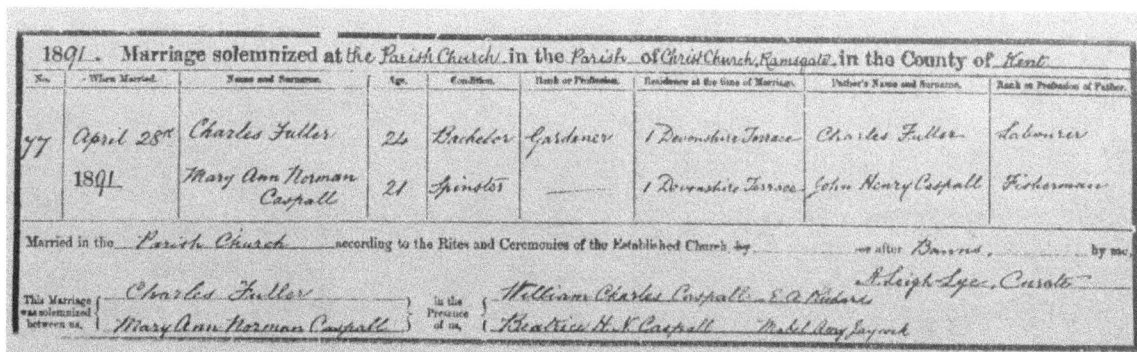

Notes

www.ingramcontent.com/pod-product-compliance
Lightning Source LLC
Chambersburg PA
CBHW081724290326
41933CB00053B/3327